# The Laugh We Make When We Fall

T0334678

## Susan Firer
### Winner of the 2001 Backwaters Prize

The Backwaters Press

Also by Susan Firer

*My Life with the Tsar and Other Poems* (New Rivers Press)
*The Underground Communion Rail* (West End Press)
*The Lives of the Saints and Everything*
                                    (Cleveland State University Poetry Center)

"Eating Pears" reprinted by permission of the University of Nebraska Press. Copyright © 1996 by the University of Nebraska Press.

All other poems Copyright © 2002 Susan Firer.

Backwaters Press Logo designed by L. L. Mannlein, Copyright © 1997, The Backwaters Press

All rights reserved. No part of this book may be reproduced in any form, except for the inclusion of brief quotations in a review, without permission in writing from the author or the publisher.

First Printing, 1000 copies, June 2002
Second Printing, 300 copies, July 2004


Published by:            The Backwaters Press
                         Greg Kosmicki, Editor/Publisher
                         3502 North 52nd Street
                         Omaha, Nebraska 68104-3506
                         (402) 451-4052
                         GKosm62735@AOL.com
                         www.thebackwaterspress.homestead.com



ISBN : 978-1-4962-2598-6

## Acknowledgements

Thanks are due to the Editors of the following magazines, in which some of the poems first appeared:

*Another Chicago Magazine:* "Blacklights" (then titled "Under Brett's Back Room Blacklights")

*Blue Moon Review:* "All Souls' Day"

*Crab Orchard Review:* "Pumpkin Seeds"

*Cream City Review:* "Whitman's Voice"; "Horse Latitudes"

*Free Verse:* "Opening the Rain"

*Georgia Review:* "Peonies"

*Hanging Loose:* "We Were in Our City"

*The Iowa Review:* "My Coat of Flowers," "Lilacs"

*Mid-American Review:* "Common Name: Scilla"

*Milwaukee Orbit:* "Permission Slips"

*North American Review:* "Hsuan T'sao"

*Oxford Magazine:* "..., ! . ?"

Prairie Schooner: "Eating Pears"

*Rattle:* "Birds"

*Southern Poetry Review:* "The Beautiful Pain of Too Much"

*Acknowledgements* (continued)

"Eating Pears" received an Honorable Mention in the National Writers Union (Santa Cruz/Monterrey Local 7) 1993 Competition, and First Place in the Writers' Place 1995 Literary Awards (Madison, Wisconsin).

"Driving Home After the Funeral" was anthologized in The Talking of Hands: A Thirtieth Anniversary Celebration, published by New Rivers Press.

"Compline" is anthologized in Jane's Stories II: An Anthology by Midwestern Women, published by Wild Dove Studio and Press.

I also wish to thank Art Futures for a Milwaukee County Artist Fellowship, which helped support the writing of this manuscript. Special thanks to David Hamilton, Stephen Corey, and Linda Aschbrenner for their generous editorial suggestions and support, and to Pam Percy, who invited me to read so many of these poems on her radio show, "Hotel Milwaukee." As always, love and thanks to James Hazard for his good ear and his incredible driving skills which often help take these poems from town to town.

Many thanks to these supporters of The Backwaters Press without whose generous contributions and subscriptions the publication of this book would not have been possible.

## ANGELS

Steve and Kathy Kloch
Greg and Barb Kuzma
Don and Marjorie Saiser
Rich and Eileen Zochol

## BENEFACTORS

Barbara and Bob Schmitz

## PATRONS

Guy and Jennie Duncan
Cheryl Kessell
Tim O'Connor
Maureen Toberer
Frederick Zydek

## SPONSORS

Paul and Mildred Kosmicki
Gary Leisman and Wendy Adams
Jeff and Patty Knag
Matt Mason
Pat Murray and Jeanne Schuler
Carol Schmid
Alan and Kim Stoler
Don Taylor

## FRIENDS

J. V. Brummels
Twyla Hansen
Judy Levin
Jim and Mary Pipher

Susan Firer

The Laugh We Make When We Fall

# CONTENTS

## Proem

Permission Slips

## Peonies

Every Thing A While  1
Peonies  3
2<sup>nd</sup> Generation  8
Compline  12
The Beautiful Pain of Too Much  14

## Blacklights

Eating Pears  19
All Souls' Day  24
Blacklights  28
We Were in Our City  29
Birds  31
My Coat of Flowers  33
Tong Yen Gai  36
The Horse Latitudes  38
Driving Home After the Funeral  41
Candlemas  43
Common Name: Scilla  44
Hsuan T'sao  46

## Ghost Poets

Lilacs  51
... , ! . ?  56
Whitman's Voice  57
Pumpkin Seeds  61
Bathing With Birds  64
Opening the Rain  66

In memory of and with love for that first family:
Ruth Lorraine Brophy Firer, Andrew Paul Firer,
Mary Catherine, and Patricia Ann

"Caves. Going down to beautiful words
descending to rosettes."

—Alice Notley, *Disobedience*

*Proem*

*Permission Slips*

My father covered in sparrows.
A Siamese triplet sunflower.
Midwest Venetian Nights.
The girl who always wears boys' Hanes briefs.
July cheerleaders throwing their bodies
      around in the heat.
South Pole explorers' cell phones.
The word *dubiety.*
The Brinks secured ashram.
The concrete sidewalk's chalked orders.
      Do a funny dance
      Do the can-can
      Do a hula.

*Peonies*

## Every Thing a While

Clothespins, *soirees*, coldcuts, planets,
Pillsbury flowers, petal pushers, grease monkeys,
Kleenex flowers, white earmuffs, zwieback,
gray & chrome dachshund-shaped electroluxes,
Godpots, dick flames, word cabinetry,
zippo flowers, thunderworms, red lipstick,
lily drop soup, skirts with pockets, fogdogs,
bunkum, glowbowling, sea butterflies,
pollen sacs, cosmological effects,
the newdeadborn, the uncle sky,
the eye in the heart, the heart in the hand,
Chinese operas, west sky Venus, garters,
horoscopy, the Contraception Museum,
Tootsie Roll Pops, relic walls, grackles,
immigrant flowers' star vowels, immigrant
birds, death certificates' filigreed frames,
juncos' algebraic flights, arborists' dreams,
movie popcorn rain in the afternoon,
a crow in a pumpkin, night high
-rise-lit office windows, bridges
of moving light, gold lamé downtowns,
spiritual careerism, leaf cassocks,

birdbaths, marsupials, slapping ghosts,
flat tires, quotation marks, fairy drinks,
the wild ride of cells, breaths' blue overcoats,
Jesus doing the hand jive, computers'
lunar nerves, UFOs' revolving doors,
brain stems, brain plates, brain storms,
bedclothes, wish bones, orange protractors of sun,
Siberian sage, *scilla siberica*, zafu
crescents. The sturdy materiality
of the memory bank, the cloud bank,
the buildings of words.

*Peonies*


The young girls walk by looking like wedding
cakes, art nouveau vases.  They are
wearing only peonies.  Exhausted
from wearing beauty, they night hurry
home to pull the flowers over their heads.
They learn that once you wear
a dress of peonies, your skin is forever
fragranced with the flowers' operatic sweet sadness.  All
over the early June city, collapsed dresses of peonies
still as rugs incense bedrooms.  Wild
canaries fly from the dresses' peony-scented puddles
and sing about the sleeping girls.


Have you heard the peonies' glossolalia?
Have you ever watched a black swallowtail's
gold and sky-blue pierced wings rearranged
by 44 mph winds, while it holds
to a Festiva Maxima Blush peony,
all the while maintaining all
its delicate migrating strength?
Have you seen your neighbor,
white-nightgowned, stop
the morning of her death

to bring greedily to her
face one last time the fragrance
of her greatly loved white Le Jours?

Looking at the sleeping new-
born in its white bassinet, one
would never believe, even if told in great detail,
what will happen to that infant during its life.
Or, if one did believe, one might go mad
with fast forwarded beauty, boredom, and terror.
Looking at the tight small gumball bud, it is
difficult to imagine the coming unfurling,
the coming foliage, the slow-opening beauty,
the insane fragrance. I watch
the drunk crazy ants come like explorers
to travel the tight white and green globes,
the holy-trinity-leaved peony buds.

All over the city, around paint-chipped garages,
around perfectly painted garages,
separating lot lines,
tied to dooryard black-iron railings,
on pillowcases and beds,
holding up houses,
in vases surrounding baths,
in the convent's oddly upright manacled bunches,

in under birdbath heavy collapsed bunches,
in vacant lots, and
reflected in witching balls,
peonies bow with fragrance
and all such burdens of beauty.

It is not hard to understand why my
immigrant grandmothers, both
the tall elegant French one and
the sweet doughy Czechoslovakian one,
prized their Limoges and cut-
glass dishes and peonies equally,
why they carried to their American homes
the promise-heavy flowers,
why they opened the soil around their new
homes and planted all the sweet
possible peonies they could find sun for,
nor why when

my mother married and moved to the new
wilderness of the suburbs she
carried the newspaper-wrapped dream
peonies with her. And I,
second generation on each family side,
have planted double-flowered Longfellow peonies

and Mrs. Franklin D. Roosevelt peonies and
Avalanche peonies all along my front steps
just so that you June visiting
might breathe in all the flowers' information,
longevity, and mad medicinal genius.

My neighbor planted her entire front yard in peonies.
In June, I am disabled with the wild sweet smell.
I cannot sleep.  Breathing in the peonies' fragrance
it is easy to understand why people wallpaper
their bedrooms with peonies, perfectly preserve
them under glass bells, try to replicate
their smell in perfumes & in house sprays,
and sleep under peony-decorated comforters.
No dreams are as wonderful as dreams
had after breathing in Queen of Hamburg peonies.
After I've breathed in nights of the truth-drug flowers,
ask me and I will tell you
about women's body memories, about
the slow, moist-opening
of peonies, the ruffled silk slippery dark-
red petals, the ant licked
open peonies, the wealthy smell of nights
of peonies that dream and swell, grow
from tightness to wild reckless
loud unfurled dropping petals.

Have you ever rubbed a peony petal
between your thumb and index finger?
It is smoother than magnolia
tongues, sweeter than yellow cake,
better than any Chinese potion.
Put a peony in your hair—
you will not be disappointed
with the suggestions whispered in your ear.

"Oatmeal was good enough for my sisters,
and they had beautiful skin.  You
don't need special soaps for washing!"

My father's job was to toughen me up
for this new world.  He had learned.
Now, he had to teach me.

He made me use brown paper toweling,
which he brought home from the brewery,
to wipe my nose when I was sick.
The house thermometer was not allowed to top

60 degrees.  Cold, 40 below wind chill
mornings, my mother warmed the kitchen
by turning on the gas stove's small campfires.

When I told my mother I wanted to pierce my ears,
she patted her shoulders with her hands, said,
"Your ears will stretch to here."

She lowered her voice:
"They'll know you're from the old country."
I wasn't from the old country,

neither were they.
Their parents were:
my father's Bohemian-speaking parents
were from Czechoslovakia.

My mother's mother
came from France, & her
father's family from Ireland.

My mother insisted on sewing
all my clothing, embroidering blouses,
zigzag rickrack decorating dresses' collars.

I wanted factory-made clothing,
not sand-colored, tissue-thin Butterick pattern
pieces spread like puzzle parts all over
our dining room table. Nights

my mother sat darning my Wigwam
soft wool crew socks,
that my penny loafers had worn

holes in the heels of.
She stretched the hole in the heel of the sock
over the top of an empty water glass.  With her

darning needle & thread she made a grid.
Moving the needle under and over the grid,
she repaired my socks while I instructed her:

*"Other kids don't wear darned socks;*
*they* throw out the ones with holes.
*They buy new ones."*  *"I never*

heard of such a thing," she'd say.
"Now you did," I'd reply.
My father could smell new shoes.

Once he had the scent he couldn't rest
until he'd sneak into my closet and steal them
off to the Russian shoe repair shop

where he had little metal crescent moons
hammered on the heels' rubber edges.
"They'll last forever," he always informed me.

I sounded like Fred Astaire tapping
my way up & down my
suburban high school's marble steps.

"*Go Go boots don't need cleats,*"
I kept telling my father, who,
as usual, repeated his own mantra:

"You wash your hair too often.
You take too many baths.
You're washing away all your body oils."

At college, like many others, I imagine,
I rebelled: NO CLEATS!
Walking in those first university snows,

away from home, in noncleated loafers, I
was startled, noticing my hardly distinguishable
from any other size 7½ girl's loafer prints.

My footprints started disappearing
into others' footprints.
I could hardly hear my own footprints.
I could hardly believe my own footprints.

# Compline

In snow we are larger than our bodies.
      On our backs,
doing horizontal jumping
      jacks, we imprint our origin.
Looking up we don't want
      to leave the satin-
creased skirts of snow.
      My son still thinks
it's only play this waiting until dark to go out
      & press our original body
outlines in streetlight lit pastures of snow.

He jokes: "Here is an abstract art angel."
      Then he falls
on his side, roots with his red-&-black checkered
      earflapped hat,
and moves his legs in scissors
runs, like a dreaming dog's sleep dream chase.
      I think we're all born
with this body memory. Even if no one ever taught us,
      we'd find ourselves,
as if in praise, allowing ourselves to fall
      backwards and
let our bodies' pregenetic body memory direct us.

We love snow because it is generous,
        decorative,     excessive,
and motherly when we fall,
        & we do
trustingly fall back into it,
        through history,
which is time and human, through
        our mother's & father's
        bodies & the bodies
of the mother & father before them.

Sometimes my son & I hold hands & fall back
        together, like skyjumpers.
Other times we watch the critical
        beauty of each others'
effort set again toward only beauty
        toward looking up & accepting
        the lake winds & pelting
snow.  We leave our bodies'
        gratitude in snow.

## The Beautiful Pain of Too Much

In the scruffle tremble
world my heart is
cake batter.  The world rattles
like a piggy bank.
Have you remembered
why you're here?
In birdheaven humans wake
in their dark houses
& lean out opened windows
to choir sing mornings to nested birds.
I am trying to tell you something
about night games,
about the soul's regattas,
and the weight of skin.
Have you ever done anything beautiful?
Beautiful as a man carrying
a French horn?  My heart
closes like an automatic garage door,
opens like a drawbridge.
We are so perfect,
so many want pretty.
We are jewel eaters,
children in bright swimming

suits crucifix falling
into Windex blue days.
Priestesses of Incan temples
wore gold sunflower medallions.
We eat sunflowers,
sit on chairs upholstered
with stars.  Can you only balance
alone?  In the depathologizing quiet,
in the pharmacology of lake,
disks of us fall, human foliose,
into the earth's green pleats.
Our spines light with fireflies.
Our hands memorize.
The body memorizes
the places of rapture,
the assemblies of devotions:
the music of cold
trees, a lisp of ice,
the butterfly forest
(Have you ever put a butterfly
in your mouth?), the aspirin sun,
our time-lapse bodies,
snow fences blown wild
with the foreign language of leaves.
The memorizing foot repeatedly
puts its steps of divination
to the fragrant dreaming earth.

*Blacklights*

*Eating Pears*


Every early fall, when the leaves still hold to the trees,
but when nights start to get cold, & I'm the only one
in the house who still sleeps with full open night
windows, and mornings, sometimes, you can see
your breath leaving your body. Only the stubborn flowers,
mums, asters, foxgloves, and cosmos, are still, & the pears,
whose noisy yellow and green growings surround
our summer lives & summer night dreams and spring
love makings, are wrapped in newspaper and
orderly as kindergarteners in the cupboard.  And
after twilight play, I call in my son
and in the lake falling jumprope purple,
gold and reds we unwrap two pears with the pleasure
of our favorite holidays (his rightfully his
birthday, mine Fat Tuesday).  We wash
the pears as you would a greatly loved child
in a Sunday night bath, when you know soon
the child will tell you he is too old for you to bathe him.
Now we wash and unwrap the pears from all
the inky headlines of the world: ethnic
cleansings and weddings, rapes and princesses,
drug house executions, stock market reports,
rescued children and bombings.  We unwrap the pears,

remembering the dreams the spring pear blossoms incensed
through our spring-screened, wide-opened windows.
Once while making love in the afternoon,
the house quiet with schooled children,
and the pear tree at its fragrance peak,
it was difficult to tell the difference
between pear blossom and human
love. We unwrap the pears we will eat,
and I remember the summer when for days
I had to be carried outside and put under
the shade love of trees, and I was fighting
to hold the baby child inside of me,
and the baby was bleeding to be gone,
and he would bring me ice, and water, and lemon,
and one night in screams and tears
he caught from my body the strange small miniature
jelly baby and put her in his hip-jacket pocket
and carried me weak bleeding to the hospital of sorrows
where I dreamt slept for days. Two summers
later just before the pears would be taken
from the tree to our house, we brought
home a new August boy baby, whom I nursed under the song
of pear leaves and the image of too-fat-soon-
to-fall pears, & the birds were all drunk with too much
of the early fallen fermented fruit, and I was drunk

with new child, and full breasts, and Chinese
lanterns that clapped in wind for all such
joys and fullnesses. We unwrap the pears
and the awful summer of confusion
where I sat not knowing myself
whether to follow the what or who,
or stay with whom? I was buried under
deaths: mother's, father's, sisters' deaths wrapped me
like surgical wrap. And who and where would I be
when all their gauzy deaths were removed?
We unwrap the pears like our sweet lives
that grow into beautiful unknown
shapes and colors, and some June fall, wind fall.
Some grow lovely bumped, soft spoiled and awkward.
After the first white slippery bite,
I make you tell me what moment
of the pear's growing you are tasting.
Because you are six, you say, "You
go first." I bite and taste and tell
of eating starlight, and lightning, and the music
of your father's cornet (Hoagy Carmichael's "Stardust")
the late summer night he played outside
the Perseids star showers and him 11 P.M.
playing outside because the summer house was
too hot to enter & there was no lake breeze,

& we sat sweaty wet in our bathing suits & the lights
of the many candles we surround ourselves in.
And now I'm telling you that I'm eating all
the lights: the alley lit by streetlight light,
music & starlight, & lightning & candle
of that night.  We bite again.
You tell me that you taste raccoon dreams
from the night the raccoons climbed up the tree
and hung their tails Davy Crockett hat-like down
through the lush leaves and starting pears.
Your memory makes me taste the song of the migrating
flock of yellow warblers that June rested in the tree.
Because you are 6, I do not tell you
but I even taste the February
pear tree of the ice frozen world, night
of my 45 year-old sister's death,
when there was not one leaf, not one pear.
All the world was frozen and covered empty,
like the pear tree that screamed the empty
inside of a mouth in an Edvard Munch painting terror.
Bix, together we are eating the hysterically clean hearts
of pears, which get sweeter & sweeter as they age.
I am 44.  Soon I will be 45.  The cupboard is filled
with carefully wrapped pears.  We are sharing
the slippery hard first bites.  We are eating pears

& our lives.  We are memorizing the lives of pears
together at the now night table we eat from.
You are 6.  You are good at this.  You tell me:
"A pear tastes nothing like it looks."
And together we blind bite, we eat our way
into the many stories of pears.

## All Souls' Day

All Souls' Day was the night
plenary indulgences were up for grabs
until midnight.  (Plenaries
remitted "All temporal
punishment due on the sins.")  On All
Souls' Day you could earn them for others.
One of the conditions required to acquire
plenary indulgences was: "that one be free
from every venial sin." (This is trickier
than it sounds, because once you know
you are not allowed one bad thought,
they just flood in: naked teachers,
forbidden words, acts of vengeance.)
There was a prayer formula: a certain number
of Our Fathers, Glory Bes,  Hail Marys
said, and you released a soul from Purgatory.
"Not that OUR family has any souls in Purgatory,"
she always told me, "just to be safe."
I pictured souls like Mary Martin's
Peter Pan shadow, but able to solo fly.
I saw them white, peacock ore iridescent.
It was always on November 2.  (All Souls' Day
is not a Movable Holy Day like the Feast

of Corpus Christi, Ascension Day or Trinity
Sunday.)  The church was always cold & damp;
people in fat overcoats huddled in prayer,
(always more women than men) kneeled
in the pews' kneelers' leather give, like flesh
islands in the great, floating continent church.
At all times a few people coughed.
And the church was always beautifully candlelit,
votives lit like wishes at the plaster feet of saints
in every hidden church corner.  The Host
would be out on the altar in the gold
sun-ray monstrance, looking like the pure eye of God.
Thick incense swung from the thurible
was everywhere.  (I was convinced it was God's own
breath that I whispered and coughed through.)
Tired from Daylight Savings Time change
and school, I'd try to use school:
"Can't we go?  I have school tomorrow!"
But she wouldn't even pause.  She'd just
keep saying her prayers, her lips moving silently,
like she was lip synching the Supremes or Martha
Reeves & The Vandellas, the whole while elbowing
elbowingandpinching me to keep me
awake until midnight when the prayers would no longer
trade out souls.  I was telling my Catholic friend

about all of this and she said,
"We don't believe in that anymore."
I said, "All Souls' Day?"
She said, "No. Purgatory."
And I was    pissed,   really angry:
All those All Souls' Days on my knees,
praying impossibly
hard, praying until I floated my child  body,
praying until the whole church glowed,
praying myself limp.  After hours
of prayer, when people finally left the church
no one's knees would straighten;
everyone's knees clicked like tumblers in
lock combinations, and everyone limped
out of church, crippled with prayer
and from dancing with the dead in snow
and incense, and candlelight, and I
just want to know, anyway, now
where do those who are not pure enough
for heaven, but not bad enough
for hell, and unbaptized babies
and all those who we were once
taught stopped over in Purgatory,
where do they go?  And, further,
what happens to a place, say a family, a marriage,
or Purgatory when no one believes in it any longer?

But possibly, just maybe, the souls
of people you were or once loved but were
too young to pray out might still be,
just might be, trapped copper beautiful there,
waiting for cold-lipped prayer litanies
to float them scallop white all the way to heaven.

## Blacklights

Dropped from the bright, hot 6 P.M. August city
sky, the white-jumpsuited, turquoise-parachuted
Elvises came skydiving down
onto a blackened-catfish smelling block-
party sidestreet, accompanied by Mrs. Fun's
8 minute rendition of "Hound Dog" – heavy
on the drums. By the time they hit earth,
the Elvises' crooked "toups" are a black mess,
their white Nikes gray, their parachute lines
a tangle. At night the young girls, who watched
the impersonators land ("Thank you very much,
thank you very much"), thank you drink
ice-cubed gin and tonics that turn
unearthly aqua colors in the bar's
blacklight back room. The women
thought they came to hear music,
but they hear poems. They remember men
who dropped from the sky,
dressed like other men who sang sequined
love songs in bed, did drugs, and promised
to pull out before they'd come, &, of course, never
did. Under the blacklight, everything white in or on
the girls shines another unearthly white.
Everything black remains altogether the same.

## We Were in Our City

We were in a different country
in our city, one where
windows had no screens—
large dark open mouths—
houses' porches were slanted
no railings to catch anyone.
And everyone was outside
in the middle of the hot night.
Inside-the-house furniture was out-
side in the dark, fat stuffed ghosts.
My sister was slapping my father
across the back of his head
with her pink slipper. Outside
the car, children were in the street,
in the dark, in their day
clothes. My sisters & I were all
in thin-summer-flowered night-
gowns & slippers. We had
been taken from our beds
to pick up our father from his work.
My father was whisper yelling
at my mother to *Quiet them down.* He
knew we shouldn't have taken

*This way.* The dog he
had just run over was wild-
ly yelping in the potholed street. A
crowd was forming around the dog
as if around some terrible truth.
My mother was thanking God
that *It wasn't some child.* My
father drove up a curb, avoiding
faces that tried to stop us.
Our gray DeSoto was a vehicle
of death, of salvation. I was
in the backseat slidebumping
onto my howling sister. Our car's
headlights were shining on places
our lives made possible,
made impossible. *They'll kill us
if we stop*, my father said,
gunning the gas, *We can't stop now.*

## Birds

I found the blue jay on the drive way
under the pink drunk Czechoslovakian-
grandma-planted peonies which were
under the restrained Scotch pine.
The bird's nape was wide open.
You could kaleidoscope look
into its neck and see rubber bands
leading to its complex brain.
You could see everywhere
it had ever flown: chaparral, scrub-oak
woodlands, coniferous, & oak forests.  There
were nuts, & insects, & seeds, & amphibians,
& even a piece or two of snake.
There was a cache of foil bright objects, &
sounds: zreeks & shook, shook, shook & all
the colors of sex and death.  I bent to it
picked it up and brought it to my heart
like the strange forest pioneer women who took
abandoned bear cubs to their bare breasts
and rocked nursed them in front
of cabin fires until the cubs could live
on their own.  I have not often since

had such patience. But then with that
found jay I stroked its wingbars & flight
feathers; I memorized its eye-rings, & crown,
wing coverts, & eye-stripes. And with weeks
and water, food, and breath
I brought it back to flight. For that
short summer, I loved it more than myself,
enough to let it go. For months it would not.
Every time I went outside, it flew streetlight
straight to my head or shoulder
where it easy perched. There are photos
of me teenage bend giving it milk blue
bowls of water and photos of me bikini sun-
bathing, the blue jay on my then
tan, flat belly, the jay feeling deceivingly
light as the first intimate gift flesh touch
of love, as the children who swell and fall
from our love-soaked bodies, deceiving
as the hollow-boned, song-filled birds
that daily blue grass drop dream feather
trails throughout our skin heavy days.

## My Coat of Flowers

This is the black velvet coat of my mother's
ballroom dancing nights.  She had it recut for me.
"Cut the ends of the sleeves pointy,
like the sleeves on the witch
in SNOW WHITE," my mother told
the kneeling, red-pincushion-braceleted dressmaker.
I was 15 and already on the runway
in a coat patterned after an apple-carrying murderer.

The sashes held me in the coat.
The milky satin lining looked like a summer planet,
a slab of freshly cut tree rings, going on
forever; it smelled like a coffin's lining.
When I put that coat on, I knew
I would invite my friends over to play
slip & slide in Tanqueray Sterling vodka.

Here was *"Un manteau de guerre."*
I scared my boyfriend half to death
in that coat. "Touch it," I told him.
"Then I will tell you what it is.
It's like nothing else.  Touch it."

"The rabat of a monsignor is purple,
that of a cardinal is red, and the Pope has
a white rabat." Me, I wore a full-dress, black coat.
The coat was a sail. On the bed, in a black puddle
you'd never imagine the stir it could create.
It was enough to make my friends forget
the Triduum of prayer celebrated on the occasion
of Saint Xavier's touring right arm,
visiting the Church of Gesu on Wisconsin Avenue.

When I put on that coat, I was all 7 dancing
princesses off in the trade winds. The coat was
a passport, a jail cell, an inky humid forest
where you knew parrotfever was prevalent.

In that coat, I could hear
every piece of galactic noise.
Diamond tiaras windchimed in trees.
Spells were being cast;
white cats were mumblety-peg dying.
Selves were unlatching. Girls with snouts
danced in the rain, in pistachio-green cutoffs.
Old men, carrying wax-paper-covered trays
of cannoli, hawked their wares and midnight
danced with black, fish-net stockinged women
half their age, without dropping
one cream-stuffed cannoli.

Are you brave enough for visions?
Concertina-barbed-wire-velvet cut hands?
Cannoli?  Trade secrets?
Once I wore a coat that made you believe
in the Virgin Birth and all other detentions
of light with their accompanying saints'
touring arms, papal bulls, and lunate bones.

In that coat I recognized that I was
the tourist of all, and I would refuse
nothing: oysters, intemperate temperatures,
aphrodisiac artichokes, and nights of knowing
nothing, no one, of course, not even
my own beautifully soft, dark-coated self.

# Tong Yen Gai

## San Francisco


The funeral procession moved past the Dragon Seed,
past the Ching Chong Dong Building, past the Buddha
Bar.  The mortuary band march-played over
the Sunday voices of commerce and pleasure.
At all places that had been important to the dead man
the chief mourners climbed out of their limousines
"to bow three times before the open hearse
as the funeral director clapped three times
to alert the drowsy spirit" to look around
one last time.  The photo on top of the hearse
was of a smiling young man.
Behind the mourners a merchant's hand
stirred a large box of live frogs.
The air was full with the fresh fish, crab,
duck, and hosed-down sidewalk smells.
I had been looking at bonsai trees and lucky,
ribbon-wrapped bamboo sticks, the spiky
awkward Durian, & porcelain erotic statues
(late Qing period), chrysanthemum teas,
brocade wrapped chopblocks and blue water-
covered moon stones.  Off in the distance
the philanthropic smell of the Pacific Ocean.  A small

boy ran by in a bright blue wisdom hat.
The store windows were full of medicinal
roots and herbs. At a traditional
Chinese funeral one should "bow 3 times
before the coffin, light a stick of incense,
and suck a piece of candy provided
to wash away the bitterness."    I rested
in front of Quang Xoung Foods.
Someone in the funeral procession released
hands full of white prayer papers.
The wind covered me with them.
They were the size of opera tickets.
Before dark I still wanted to see
Beniamino Bufano's statue of Sun Yat-Sen,
I wanted to get to the Sue Hing Benevolent Association.
I wanted to climb to the top floor Tin How Temple
of the Goddess of Heaven, protectoress of all sojourners.

## The Horse Latitudes

*"These zones...are the breeding grounds*
*of many of the world's strange winds"*

In the book of winds & wings
there are blue women
who shiver their wings out
to extraordinary size, unfurled
into commonality, monkey-vanilla
see through.  Everything,
every thing is made up of 12 particles.
Of blue, in the book of wings,
there are women with skyscraper wings,
women with bruised wings, blue heron
wings, women with orchid fuck wings.
There are women with blue birth wings
that turn red then flesh, or not,
when hit with air, women with blue
milk wings, women with gunmetal wings.
There are women whose wings cradle
& rock the lonely suicides &
dig their places of burial.  There are
women who spread their wings across cold
wood floors, line graves with their ice satin
wings, let other people walk across them,

sleep in them, chew on them.  There are
women who set their wings on fire & fly
comet beautiful in the corner of sight,
& women whose crushed wings turn air
to spice.  There are women with wings
of toast who eat their own wings, & others
who feed their scallop wings to others.
Have you ever smelled a blue wing?
Heard a show tune wing?
Licked a licorice one?  There are women
with brass in their wings & women
with stained glass wings.  Women
are dressing in winds & maps & wings.
There are wings shaped like breasts,
and breasts that are wings, & if you drink,
you fly scared, raved, smashed, & crushed.
Touch the hyacinth-blue bloom of woman
wing, iris blue, dirt blue, finger-stain blue.
A powder-blue winged and capped grandma
walks her Tartan-plaid sweatered,
white westies through the village
April snowstorm.  There is beauty
in those milk-white-blue
beautifully embossed wings.
In the BOOK OF ANGELS, there are angels
known to have 6 wings.  In the book of winds &

wings, there are days of wings, skies of wings.
You don't always like your poor-white-blue-glue wings
always catching and covered with the past,
like decals on Winnebagoes, tags
on trans-Atlantic luggage, cockleburs?
There are others: wings of ether & African
violet wings, champagne wings, first communion
wings.  In the flammable air
the shape and cargo of wings
ramp & run the dimensions of whim,
of lightning (ball, bolt, & eye).  Have you seen
the swath of wings?  Heard them stir?   Fallen
wing deep in the names of winds?
Waff, Black Roller, Erh Chi Chih Fung,
Williwaw, Sz, Om, Chwa, Tsumuji.  Always
such thin boundaries between skin & the celestial
radio's God voice ghosting all the blue
winds & wings.

## Driving Home After the Funeral

We stopped outside Lake Geneva.
At a plywood produce stand,
we asked to go out into
the pumpkin field. The 3 of us
stood there in our holy confused lives
in the tripping vines,
among the startling
brilliant shapes and
oranges of pumpkins. Grief
is a toll road, a large field. If you listen
closely, each pumpkin speaks a name.
We stood raw with loss
in the erupting fields of color
under the still warm, late October
sun. (October, the month of rosaries.)
Our feet released the songs of the buried.
We were greedy with loss, grabbing
the pumpkins by their prickly stems,
and loving the pain of it. We stopped
there in the wilderness of loss & pumpkins.
We had just buried your mother.

Our son, & you, & I were the only
people in the weekday pumpkin field.
We were separating
pumpkins from their vines.
We were snapping
the prickly stems
from their tangled vines.
We were taking more than we needed.
We held the pumpkins close to our bodies,
loving their awkward weight & dirt smell.
We held the odd Laurel
& Hardy shaped ones, the movie
starlet perfect ones, the accordion
pleated pumpkins, the green
ones, the candle-flame-colored
ones, the pumpkins that flat leaned
to the dirt they came from, &
the pumpkins that grew lonely
next to the papery cornstalks at the edge
of the field.  It was so windy
our hair whipped our faces.  It seemed
the wind was blowing the world away.  All,
except the pumpkins and us who stood
loss-full, wrapping ourselves around the beautiful
flesh and seeds of autumn
held in the fields of pumpkins.

## Candlemas

Out in the winter garden
there's only this survivor of blizzards:
the snowdrop, *galanthus nivalis,*
ancient altar scatter, milkflower,

the lonely-as-Jesus flower
with all its survivor ecstasies.

The French called the flower *perce-neige,*
      piercing the snow.
The ancients made amulets
      of its white-belled tepals.

Who wouldn't?
A flower that survives repeated late-heavy snows
then takes on and makes lovely
the color of what it survives.

*Common Name: Scilla*
     *Genus Name: Scilla*
     *Type: Perennial*


Under the slingshot birches,
under the herring gulls' cries
the ground is thick blue
with the bright spikes of scilla.
John Gerard, author of a 16th century herbal,
wrote about scilla: "...small bleu
flowers consisting of sixe little leaves
spread abroad like a star.  The seed
is contained in small round bullets."
Scilla surrounds the rocks.
The rocks are all intelligence,
are documents, lit in a way
we can see everything once we've been
completely lost.  The scilla are
so beautiful; I always feel
rich when I walk on them.  Always
everywhere there are rafts of broken and
flowers bright as headlights.  The migrating
Lepidoptera have club-shaped antennae
and straw like proboscis.  At the museum
I read that Lepidoptera drink animal tears.
Once I saw a man with butterfly horns.

For a while the sky memories us about
like primary-colored beach balls.
The trees give us dreams; they lay
down shadows dark with memory.
The scilla grow wild there.
The Welsh call scilla "cuckoo's boots."
Scilla are beautiful but poisonous.
In Europe red scilla was used as rat poison.
Today on his way home from Lake
Geneva, I asked my husband
to bring a malt-cup-silver pail full of wild
scilla for me to plant in our yard.
Sometimes on my morning lake run I do
the scilla mantra. Every time I step
down on the ball of my right foot
I say scilla. Scilla. Scilla.
The genus name for scilla is scilla
which means "I injure." Often I mantra
that: *I injure I injure I injure*

*Hsuan T'sao*

The early July midwest yards
are full of the Dalai Lama-robed flowers;
garages float in their flames.

Before the flowers made their way
along the Oriental Silk Route to here,
pregnant Chinese women wore them
in their gowns "to insure the birth

of sons." I admire
the stems' generosity
of blossoms: always several and

the way the stems reach
past their origin, carrying secrets
up from the dark earth and turning
them to bright-star-filled flowers.

In Spring the Chinese ate day lily buds,
believing them a tonic to lessen grief.
They called the flower *hsuan t'sao*:

"the flower of forgetfulness."  They dried
and stored the Viceroy-colored blossoms.
I surround my own summer
table with a slew of the rayed

flowers.  In July I serve visitors
exquisite dips in the flowers' edible drug.
Together we eat the delicate rust

blossoms of brevity and forgetfulness.

*Ghost Poets*

## Lilacs

Before his doctor cut into his
7<sup>th</sup> cervical disk,
like an old Swede's goat he clumped
climbed the black garage roof next door
thump thump to throw
down on me the lightest, most
fragrant bunches of lilacs.  I lusted
for the lilacs, the drunk
lilacs, the purple flabellum,
spodumene, sumptuous benedictional lilacs,
the Nerudian excessive lilacs.
Neruda's desk came to him from a wave
off Isla Negra.  "Matilde! Matilde!
My desk!  My desk!" he yelled,
spotting the wood in the ocean.
Together Matilde and Neruda
"went down to the beach and sat
on the sand, waiting for a wave
to wash up the wood...."
Neruda placed the wood ocean view
in front of a window and placed
a photo of young Whitman on it &
a photo of old Whitman on it.

How Whitman loved lilacs.  You can
smell lilacs when you read Whitman.
Breathing lilacs our house falls dark
around us, drops like night clothing
days' faces.  Convalescent-hearted
lilac pilgrims cannot stop breathing
the wet dark lilac nights.
Put a bed of lilacs down
and I will meet you.  We will not sleep.
Friends all over are falling.
There are so many ways to fall.
Lilacs offer their transfusions.
In the Houghton Mifflin New
College Edition of *American Heritage*
*Dictionary of the English*
*Language*, on page 757 (like/limb),
they show photos of the perfectly-postured
lily & the very well-behaved lily
of the valley.  What about lilacs?  I write
the editors.  What about scratch & sniff lilacs?
All over late May, lilacs like burglars
surround outbuildings,
& houses, & hospitals, & bus stops.
(On your way to your morning
bus, if you stop to pick Gabriel's lilacs,
you will miss your bus.)

Lilacs heal lovers'
quarrels, and I swear they floated
the ship from Singapore
anchored outside our Memorial
Day lake breakwater,
making the huge ship look
like a ghost ship,
floating on lilac water.  You
already know a lot about a girl
if you see her carrying a sprig of lilacs,
if she tucks a sprig in her hair,
if she bathes in an evening tub
full of lilacs and water.
Night commendatory lilacs brush
the windows with lavender stars
of fragrance.  Dirigibles
of lilacs cover us beautifully
as a garden's bell cloche.
I raise my lilac scratched arms
for the mammogram lady.
She arranges my breasts on her
just spray cleaned plastic plate
like cut flowers.  I believe in evening
she might be giving a formal dinner.
So much is conjecture,
subjective, history.

In the Downer Theatre yellow-starred,
emerald-green-tiled ticket booth,
the ticket seller sits like a fortune
teller.  She has put a wavy-script sign
in her window.  It reads: HOLD ON
TO YOUR MONEY OR IT WILL BLOW AWAY.
It should read: LILACS ARE ALWAYS
LOVELY.  They sign pleasure (On our
dark, night living
room floor, he surrounds me with lilacs
& whispers, "Now you mustn't move").
Tulips & pumpkins trip me.
I feel misplaced as poodles
in Lake Michigan.  Poodles in Lake Michigan!
My mother told me I was mailed to earth
in an envelope of lilacs,
there is not one reason to disbelieve her.
In lilac days, my mouth full
of ripe, yellow starfruit,
I swallow and listen to the already almost
lilium & tomatoes & delphiniums &
the always too brief flowering lilacs.
In the dark I sneak
out on the soft, moon shine yarrow-
yellow-caterpillar-like seed softened
sidewalks.  I stand pelted by soft

green maple seed wings that helix fall
wind whip to earth. (In sunlight
the children will split & wear
on their noses the same winged seeds.)
I stand in the ample
lilacs, the only flower with enough
fragrance to convert everyone
in the city to crime.
Dorothy visited the Emerald City. Yearly
I surrender myself to the unrestrained
wash rabble lilacs,
the windy caravan of lilacs,
the narcoleptic steambath
invitation of lilacs.

*... , ! . ?*

> period?
> colon?
> space??
>                     — Ted Berrigan


They found Amelia Earhart's bones  (!) (.) (?)
                A sextant was next to them (...) (?)
                                What (?)  Snow smells (.) (?) (:)
Do you ever need a bratwurst (!) (?)
4 (.) (:) 44
Fish don't have vocal cords (.) (!) (?)
                They serenade with their fish bladders (?) (.) (!)
Should we got old (,) (?)
Underwater
                silver perch cluck like chickens (.) (!)
                Shrimp crackle like bacon (.) (!)
Look out (.) (!)
No one is who we want them to be
                for very long (!) (.) (?)

## Whitman's Voice

He does not sing the poem like Yeats
reciting "The Lake Isle of Innisfree";  he
simply continent speaks each word, & in between
each bump on the wax cylinder recording
Thomas Edison made of Whitman in 1890,
you hear another Whitman.

You hear Whitman
        interviewing P.T. Barnum,
        with Tom Thumb & the orangutan,
        Mlle. Jane, in the background.
You hear all the gaslight
        drenched operas he attended
        & even smell the peculiar
        19th century perfumes.
You hear Whitman's
        body kicks & swim splash & cold water scrubs
        at Gray's Swimming Bath at the bottom
        of Fulton Street, and
You hear him
        at the corner of Fulton & Cranberry Streets
        in the Rome brothers' print shop
        setting the type for the first
        *Leaves of Grass.*

You hear all
            the Nor'easters he sat outside through
            under his tree in the healing country
            under his gray wool blanket
            recovering from a stroke, and
You can even hear the Civil War
            hospital kisses he soft lip-pressed on the often
            never-shaved cheeks of the dying
            soldiers he nursed.
You hear him ask them: "Stamps?
            Licorice?
            Can I write a letter home for you?"


And in his American-formed voice inflected with canaries,
            locomotives, and turkeys,
            you hear electricity & his wild throat
            muscles.  Each syllable is a tableau:
Six year old Walter in the arms of Lafayette,
young teacher Walter playing baseball with his students,
Whitman at Poe's reburial in Baltimore
            (the only literary figure to attend),
            Walter in Brooklyn purchasing his first
            silver watch, gold pencil, frock coat,
            & loud singing on top an omni-
            bus in New York.
You see Whitman in the Astor Library

blowy from the ferry, a copy of *Consuelo*
in his hands, a bit of George Sand's
cigar smoke about his ears & beard.
You see coffee & beefsteak eating Walt &
1857 hard pressed for money Walt
watching his Talbot painting and his
few other belongings taken by lawyers
& carried out & through the streets –
all for a $200 debt.
You see Walt visiting
with brown velvet-suited Oscar
Wilde, with Longfellow, with Thoreau,
&, of course, with Emerson.
There's Walt swimming & loping at Coney Island
& writing: "The polka increases in popularity,"
& even (I am *not* making this up) walking
& loving walking the streets of Milwaukee!
You see nude sun-bathed, mud-bathed lame Walt
at Timber Creek wrestling with saplings
trying to strengthen his stroke-weakened
arms & legs.
You even see old white-bearded Whitman
napping in his wheelchair
in front of his Mickle Street Camden window,
like a "great old Angora Tom,"
like a snowy owl.

And in each syllable, you hear transformation.
        You hear his dream
        breath, his sighs
        as he studies the night
        sky patterns, hieroglyphics,
        phrenology, & lexicology.
You hear him call through the centuries
        to all his young apprentices:  "Hen,
        oh, why, Hen."
And if you are very still when listening,
        you can hear him rubbing lilacs
        in his beautiful, white beard, & I swear,
        you can hear him swallow a strawberry.


Here, on my CD made from Edison's wax cylinders
is sapling planting Walt,
America's great slang coloratura
word hero, plainly speaking; venerable Walt
saying his hymn of vowels & consonants.
And really his voice is much like the Long Island
pond and spring water he wrote about:
"The water itself has a character of its own,"
said Whitman, "It is deliciously sweet
—it almost has a flavor."

## Pumpkin Seeds

All day they are in the dark of my purse,
shocking against my hip, white
flame-shaped coins,

quiet as nonagenarians,
bright as brainjewels, secret
as a parent's dead body.

After dinner, I go behind the house
to the dark compost pile, where I turn under all
the leftovers: coffee grounds, egg shells, grass
clippings, dead sisters, dandelions.

I turn all into black dirt
and make six twelve-inch mounds of compost.
I cover those with top-soil,

and soak them with the collected rainwater.
When the mounds are black wet,
with my index finger, I poke
the small white ghosts

back into the dark wet home-
made dirt. The seeds keep sticking
to my fingers & palms.

At night when I try to fall
asleep, I think the stories of all
I've planted. I think of the small
white ghost seeds sticking to my hands.

The pumpkin seed package says let germinate
for 7-10 days. Then thin to 3 or 4 vines
per mound. The seeds are like magnets;
they pull me to their mounds to watch

for the moment when they'll green push
out of the dark. Not all make it.
After comes the hard as God job of
thinning, deciding which vines live,

which get yanked & shoveled back into
the compost. It took me a long time to be
able to do the necessary thinning out—
removing a few in order to let

the others flourish. Does God tire
of these decisions? Sometimes, like me,
does he make mistakes? Pull a handful
of flowers? The wrong angel-leaved seedling?

Then it's all waiting. I'm Darwinian
about what survives & what doesn't. Pretty
quickly the seedlings lose their angel
leaves & become more complicatedly leaved

& beautifully bright orange flowered.
I love the vines' jubilarian flowers
as much as the pumpkins. I'd plant seeds
for them alone. Whenever

I read a rhapsodic poem, say the dictionary or
Walt Whitman, whenever I see a tended garden,
I can't help it: I always assume the person who
made it has some deep acquaintance with despair.

## Bathing with Birds

After dinner all the open Chang-Cheng,
white carry-out container tops
looked like origami cranes.
In the garden the toads
pulled their finished skins off
delicately as evening gloves.
The lake wrote
contracts of chrome spume glint.
While I soaked,
birds sharpened their beaks
on the windowsill like you would knives
on the evening before a holiday.
The night sky filled with Chagall
topsy-turvy floating men & women.
I had never bathed with birds before.
I couldn't take my eyes off the emperorish
cardinal, the way he spread his tomato-colored
tail feathers in fortunes.  The starling's
lovely wing spray felt like a man's hungry
pinches, small February hailstones,
the gravel of ground gemstones.
I thought of St. Michael's armor
turning to feathers.  St. Francis and St. Clare

finally delivering their bodies to one another.
The tantric wing-spread movement,
the song moans,
beaks decorated and softened
with petals of daffodils,
the cello-music of their throats,
the blue slapping of coverts and primaries—
feathers floating in bath-
water, on the bed, in air,
in underthings, on the yellow soap.
I opened the bathing room's window—
below a black-mini-skirted,
red-high-heeled man ran
under the powerlines, through
the lilac-wallpapered alley,
wearing a red hat which greatly
resembled the Buddha's
cranial bump flame of wisdom.

## Opening the Rain

We return covered with the carnivalesque
rains' information.  We're always
up for a miracle: a godbath,
an unraveling of the dead.  Out the window
the fire-epauletted blackbirds perform
lake aerial acts, architectures
of desire and destruction.  Houses hold
histories, everything tethered to consonants
and vowels.  I underestimated
years, the viney laws of governments,
the violence of wealth, and crowds
of loneliness.  Each floorboard's a song,
a curfew.  The world writes
its own poetry in chrysanthemums.
We rewrite in hours.  Every thing
was once made up.  Love
is voodoo, prayer a cosmetic.  Here
finches fly from under covers.
Cello strings turn to fragrance.
Sleeping we understand we are never
the same.  Even the trees' branches seem jealous

of all this.  They break
through awnings and screens
reach through language's bright wrapping paper
into the dark religions of our lives.

Susan Firer grew up along the western shore of Lake Michigan, where she now lives, writes, and works. She is the author of three previous books of poetry. Her third book, THE LIVES OF THE SAINTS AND EVERYTHING, won the Cleveland State Poetry Prize and Posner Award. Her work has appeared in numerous magazines and anthologies, including *The Best American Poetry, Georgia Review, Prairie Schooner, Chicago Review, Iowa Review, New American Writing*, and others. She has read her poems widely in the Midwest, on public radio and television. For many years she worked with the Great Lakes Poem Band, a collaborative effort joining poems and music. She teaches in the creative writing program at the University of Wisconsin-Milwaukee.

Susan Firer

Lightning Source UK Ltd.
Milton Keynes UK
UKHW012040081022
410021UK00014B/395